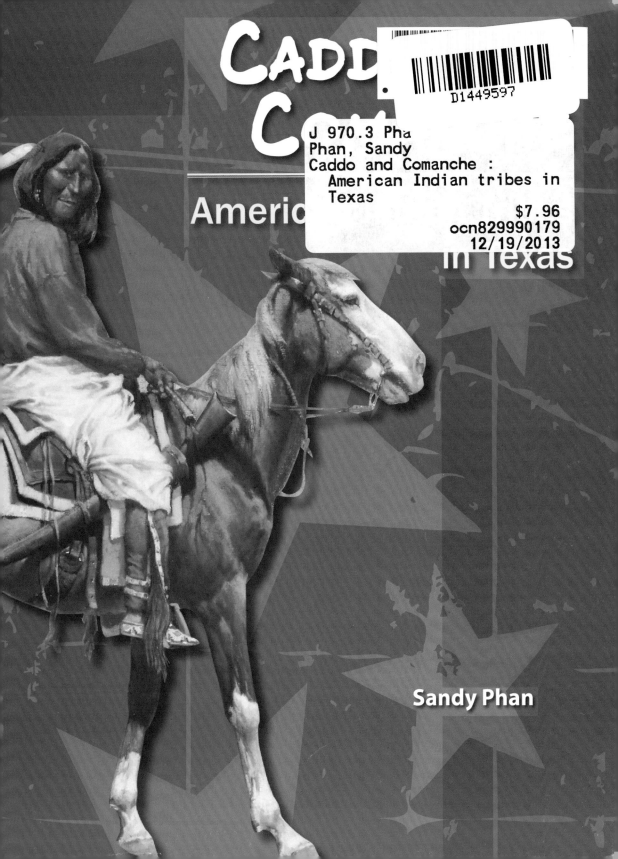

CADDO and COMANCHE

American Indian Tribes in Texas

Sandy Phan

Consultant

Devia Cearlock
K–12 Social Studies Specialist
Amarillo Independent School District

Publishing Credits

Dona Herweck Rice, *Editor-in-Chief*
Lee Aucoin, *Creative Director*
Marcus McArthur, Ph.D, *Associate Education Editor*
Neri Garcia, *Senior Designer*
Stephanie Reid, *Photo Editor*
Rachelle Cracchiolo, M.S.Ed., *Publisher*

Image Credits:
Cover National Geographic Stock & Bridgeman Art
Library; p.1 Bridgeman Art Library; pp.2–3 National
Geographic Stock; p.4 The Granger Collection;
p.5 Bridgeman Art Library; p.5 (sidebar) Randy
Mallory for Texas Historical Commission; p.6 National
Geographic Stock; p.7 The Granger Collection;
p.8 (left) Nativestock Pictures; p.8 (right) Alamy;
p.9, 10 Nativestock Pictures; p.11 (left) Nativestock
Pictures; p.11 (right) The Granger Collection;
p.12, 13 Nativestock Pictures; p.14 Album/Oronoz/
Newscom; p.15 Nativestock Pictures; p.15 (sidebar)
Northwind Picture Archives; pp.16–17 SuperStock;
p.17 National Archives; p.19 (top) Jeri Redcorn;
p.19 (bottom) Associated Press; p.20 (sidebar) akg–
images/Newscom; p.20 Nativestock Pictures; p.21 (left)
Nativestock Pictures, (right) akg–images/Newscom;
p.22 LOC [LC–USZC4–6878]; p.23 KRT/Newscom;
p.23 (sidebar) Nativestock Pictures; pp.24–25 The
Granger Collection; p.25 Bridgeman Art Library;
p.26 Corbis; p.27 Uyvsdi/Wikimedia; p.27 (sidebar)
Caddo Nation Museum; p.28 (top) Associated Press;
p.28 (bottom) AFP/Newscom; p.29 Nativestock
Pictures; All other images Shutterstock.

Teacher Created Materials
5301 Oceanus Drive
Huntington Beach, CA 92649-1030
http://www.tcmpub.com
ISBN 978-1-4333-5041-2
© 2013 Teacher Created Materials, Inc.

Table of Contents

Lost Earth

They honored the sun and moon. They listened to the spirits of animals. They believed the spirits brought healing and power in war. But one day, new people arrived from another land. These strangers believed they had the right to take the land and kill the animals.

The Caddo (KAHD-doh) and Comanche (kuh-MAN-chee) were two of the largest American Indian tribes in Texas. These American Indians fought each other. They also made **alliances** (uh-LAHY-uhns-iz) and traded with other tribes. All American Indian tribes honored the earth. But Europeans thought they could own the earth. These new settlers threatened the American Indians' way of life.

The Comanche were skilled horsemen.

The Caddo tried to live in peace with white settlers. They became traders among Europeans and other tribes. The Comanche were a more warlike people. They fought with others over hunting grounds. Over time, almost all of the original American Indian tribes in Texas died from war or disease. The few survivors were moved to **reservations**. Reservations are protected lands that are set aside just for American Indians.

a Caddo man's profile fashioned in copper

Children from the Caddo Nation stand in front of a Caddoan Mound.

Caddoan Mounds

Around the year 800, the Caddo built a city in East Texas around two temples. They often burned the temples and built new ones over them. They buried leaders nearby. The three large ritual mounds still stand at the Caddoan Mounds State Historic Site.

Ghost Dance

Wovoka (wuh-VOH-kuh), or Jack Wilson, began the Ghost Dance religion in 1889. He preached about a new Earth without white men. He said the spirits of dead American Indians and bison would return. A new earth never came. But the Caddo and other tribes still hold Ghost Dances to preserve their culture.

The Caddo
Caddo Origins and Society

The early Caddo lived in East Texas from AD 700 to 1300. They built villages around temples on top of earthen mounds. They were hunters, fishers, and gatherers. Later Caddo groups became expert farmers.

Caddo people were **matrilineal** (ma-truh-LIN-ee-uhl). This means that clan, or group, names are passed from a mother to her children. Most Caddo leaders were men who inherited their jobs. Each village had a *xinesi* (she-NAY-see), or head priest, who led religious ceremonies. Medicine men called *connas* (kon-ah) healed sick people. A *caddi* (ka-ha-DI), or chief, and village elders made rules.

Caddo village

6

Caddo chief

There were many Caddo tribes, but three **confederacies** (kuhn-FED-er-uh-seez), or unions, remain. The Hasinai (ha-SIN-ay) lived in East Texas. Their word for "friend" — *taysha* — later became the word *Texas*. The Natchitoches (nah-shi-TOSH) lived in Louisiana. The Kadohadacho (kah-do-ha-DAH-cho) lived at the borders of Texas, Oklahoma, and Arkansas. The French shortened the name to *Caddo*. This term is now used to describe all the tribes that spoke the Caddoan language.

Place of Crying

The Caddo believe that all people used to live in darkness underground. A Caddo man led his villagers toward a light in a cave. But some people were trapped below the ground. The Caddo call the place where the first people came into the world *Cha'kani'na* (cha-KAH-nee-nah). It means "place of crying."

Caddi Ayo

The supreme god of the Caddo was Caddi Ayo (ka-ha-DI HA-yo). The Caddo believed twin boys received messages from Caddi Ayo. They told these messages to the *xinesi* who passed them on to the Caddo people. Many American Indian myths and religions include twins.

Caddo Children

Caddo children helped with chores. Boys learned how to make tools and weapons. Girls learned how to make pottery, baskets, and clothing. Women also taught girls how to cook. Children listened to stories about Caddo culture from village elders.

dried corn

Corn

Corn was a very important crop. The Caddo dried corn on the cob, used the seeds for planting, and ground dried corn into flour for bread. Raw corn was cooked in stews with meat and beans. The Caddo also traded corn for bison meat and horses. They had corn-planting ceremonies and celebrated after a good harvest.

Caddo Daily Life

The Caddo homeland was the Red River Valley. This is where Texas, Louisiana, Oklahoma, and Arkansas meet. The Caddo **worshipped** and held meetings on temple mounds at the village center. They built cone-shaped houses out of wooden poles and grass mats. A fire burned inside each home for cooking and warmth. The Caddo also used animal skins to stay warm.

Caddo house

Caddo man in ceremonial clothing

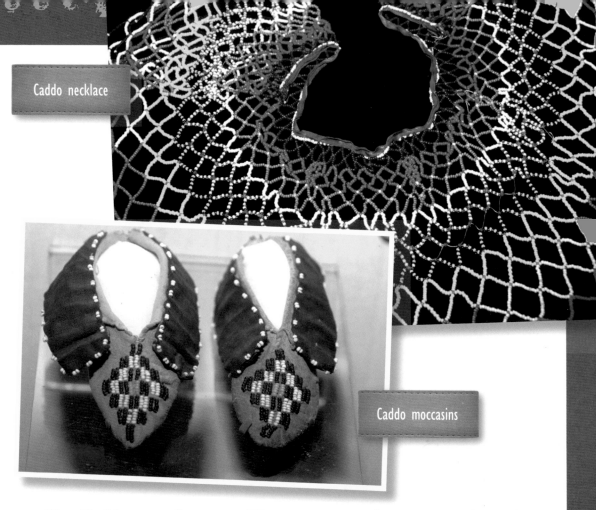

Caddo necklace

Caddo moccasins

The Caddo were farmers. They grew corn, beans, squash, and tobacco. Caddo men also were hunters and warriors. They used bows and arrows, knives, and clubs. They fished and hunted bison, deer, and other animals. Caddo women gathered wild plants. They dried vegetables, fruit, and meat. They also made baskets and clay pots to store the food. Everyone built houses and planted and harvested crops. They joined together for feasts and ceremonies.

Caddo men wore **breechcloths**, and the women wore dresses. The Caddo protected their feet with **moccasins** (MOK-uh-sinz), or shoes made out of animal hide. Some men wore their hair in a **mohawk**, which is a long strip down the center of their head.

The Comanche
Comanche Origins and Society

The Comanche are a group within the Shoshone (shoh-SHOH-nee) people. They were hunters and gatherers in the mountain forests of the central Northwest. In the 1700s, they moved south to the plains, where they became expert horsemen and warriors. They ruled a large area in western Oklahoma and Texas called the *Comanchería* (koh-mahn-che-REE-uh).

Comanche drawing of a bison hunt

The Comanche were **nomadic** people, moving around in search of bison. They lived in small family groups called *bands*. There were around 13 major Comanche groups. The *Penateka* (pen-ah-TUH-kuh), or "honey eaters," were the first group to move south. The *Kwahadi* (KWAH-ha-duh), or "antelope," lived in West Texas. The *Nokone* (no-KOH-nee), or "wanderers," moved around east Comanchería.

Comanche warrior

Comanche war shirt

Friend or Foe?

The Comanche called themselves *numunu* (NUH-muh-nuh), meaning "the people." But the word *comanche* came from the Ute (yoot) tribe's word for "enemy." The Spanish also saw the Comanche raiders as enemies and called them "Komántcia" (koh-MAHN-shi-uh).

Comanche Customs

Comanche men wore breechcloths and moccasins with ankle flaps. They braided their hair and painted their scalps along the part. Warriors painted their faces and bodies before battle. They put bison horns, feathers, and beads in their hair. Women wore buckskin dresses decorated with paint, beads, or **tinkling** metal.

Comanche bands were led by a peace chief, a war chief, and a council. Peace chiefs were wise men who advised the bands. War chiefs only led during times of war. All adult men took part in band councils.

Comanche Daily Life

Comanche bands stayed in camps near streams. The women did most of the work in camp. They took care of young children. They built cone-shaped houses called **tepees** (TEE-peez). They sewed clothes, cooked, and gathered firewood and wild plants.

Comanche men were good hunters. They tracked bison, elk, and bears. Comanche warriors fought to protect their hunting grounds. They raided their enemies for horses and food. They killed the men and captured women and children. The women became slaves, and some of the children were adopted into the band.

Children were very important to the Comanche. New members made bands stronger, especially boys. They learned how to hunt and make bows and arrows. Women taught girls how to sew and cook. Both boys and girls learned how to ride horses.

Comanche tepee and travois

Comanche arrowhead made from stone and attached to the end of a spear

The band chief and his council decided when a band should move. Comanche women would make a **travois** (truh-VOI), or sled, out of tepee poles and bison skin. They would pack the travois and unload it at the next campsite.

Comanche saddle

Waste Nothing

The Comanche used every part of a bison. They ate its meat and organs. Women used the skin for tepees and clothing. They carried water in bison stomachs. Bones and horns made tools. Sinew, or tendons, became thread and bowstrings. Tough rawhide made saddles, moccasin soles, and drums.

Vision Quest

The Comanche believed each person had "medicine," or spiritual power. Every young man had a vision quest, or spiritual journey. He went into the hills alone for four days. The spirits sent him a vision that gave him spiritual powers. Men needed strong medicine to win battles and hunt.

Contact with Europeans

In the 1500s and 1600s, the Caddo and Comanche met Spanish and French explorers. These strangers changed the American Indians' way of life.

The Spanish first brought horses to New Mexico and Texas in the 1500s. In 1680, Pueblos forced the Spanish out of New Mexico. The Spanish left many horses behind on the plains. The Comanche became the best horse riders in North America. Horses allowed the Comanche to travel farther. They waged war with many tribes and ruled the plains. The Caddo also learned how to ride horses but stayed close to their villages.

Comanche with a fur trader

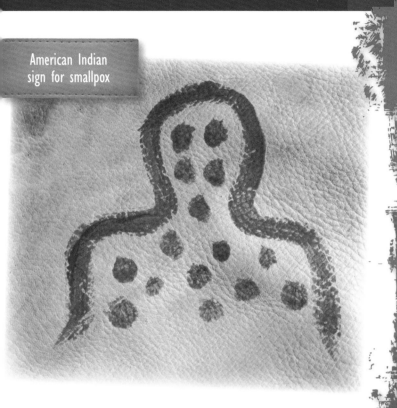

René-Robert de La Salle

The Caddo and Comanche traded with the Spanish and French. They traded animal hides for horses, guns, metal tools, and cooking pots. The men began to wear leather shirts after they met European traders. Apache (uh-PAH-chee) tribes often helped the Spanish fight Comanche raiders in Texas.

The Europeans also brought new illnesses. By the late 1700s, half of the Caddo had died from foreign diseases like **smallpox**.

Accidental Discovery

In 1682, René-Robert de La Salle (ruh-NEY roh-BEAR dyoo luh sahl) claimed the Mississippi River Valley for France. He planned to start a **colony** near the river in Louisiana. But his ship got lost and landed in Texas, where he built Fort Saint Louis. Some of his men married Caddo women and lived with the tribe. La Salle was killed before he found the Mississippi River.

Horses

The Comanche used horses for hunting and raiding. Horses also helped with moving camp and gathering food. Owning many horses meant a Comanche man was wealthy.

Americans Arrive

In the 1800s, many Americans headed west to Texas. They took land from the Caddo, Comanche, and other tribes living there.

In 1803, France sold the Louisiana Territory to the United States. But the Louisiana Purchase never set a clear border between Texas and Louisiana. In 1821, Texas became Mexican territory. Mexico and the United States fought over Caddo land. The Santa Fe Trail opened that same year, bringing even more Americans into Caddo land.

At first, Americans mostly stayed off the Comanchería, but they took control of Texas in 1836. Soon, a flood of American settlers arrived. They built houses and forts on Comanche hunting grounds. The Comanche raided white settlements. The United States and Comanche could not make lasting peace. The Comanche would not give up their land, and the United States refused to enforce a boundary between the Comanchería and American settlements.

This map shows the Louisiana Territory.

The Comanche attack a wagon train.

Sabine River

Many Caddo lived along the Sabine (SUH-bean) River. The Spanish claimed that the land around the Sabine was part of Texas. The French believed it was part of Louisiana. In 1806, the United States and Spain agreed to set the Texas-Louisiana boundary along the Sabine River.

Council House Fight

In 1840, Comanche and Texas leaders gathered for a meeting. Texas wanted the Comanche to return all captives and stop raiding white settlements. But the Comanche peace chief did not have control over all Comanche bands. Texas soldiers arrived and a fight broke out. When the Council House Fight ended, 35 Comanche were dead.

Tribal Relations
The Caddos and Their Neighbors

For years, the Caddo mostly enjoyed peace with other tribes. They lived in open areas without **fortified** gates. The Caddo were famous traders. Many tribes came to trade with them. The Spanish in New Mexico learned about the Caddo from the Jumano (hoo-MAH-noh). The Caddo traded pottery, bows, corn, and salt. They received shells and **turquoise** (TUR-koiz) from as far west as California.

In the 1700s and early 1800s, the Caddo had to fight off many other American Indian groups. Tribes arrived from the north and east, such as the Osage, Choctaw (CHOK-taw), and Chickasaw. These rival American Indian groups had guns. They came to Caddo land to escape American settlers. Apache and Comanche horsemen from the west raided Caddo villages. The Caddo had trouble fighting off attackers because they had been weakened by European diseases.

The Caddo became trade partners with the French. Other tribes traded animal skins, horses, and Apache slaves through the Caddo. The Caddo traded them French guns and European goods.

turquoise rocks

Jeri Redcorn

Jeri Redcorn pottery

Jeri Redcorn

Jeri Redcorn is a modern Caddo woman who saw ancient Caddo pottery in a museum. She wanted to learn how to make these pieces, but nobody had made this kind of pottery for a long time. So, she taught herself this lost art of her ancestors. As she makes these pieces, she thinks about her Caddo ancestors. She thinks about what tools they might have used and what their lives were like.

Some **archaeologists** (ahr-kee-OL-uh-jists) have asked Redcorn to copy ancient pieces. They buy her pottery to show in museums. Redcorn also teaches others the Caddo craft so it will never again become a lost art.

Chief Quanah Parker

Quanah Parker

Quanah (KWAH-nuh) Parker was a famous Comanche leader. His mother was a white captive and had become part of the Kwahadi band. Quanah's father was a war chief. Quanah became the Kwahadi chief. He led the battle against bison hunters. He also helped spread the Native American Church religion.

Counting Coup

American Indian warriors showed bravery in battle by "counting coup." Counting coup meant touching an enemy during a fight. For many tribes, counting coup was a way to win without killing too many men. But the Comanche killed most of the men they touched. They also took **scalps** as proof of counting coup.

Comanche Enemies and Allies

The Comanche were a warlike people, fighting over hunting grounds with many American Indian tribes. They were known as the fiercest warriors on the plains.

The Comanche drove the Mescalero (mes-kuh-LAIR-oh) and Jicarilla (hee-kuh-REE-uh) Apache out of Texas. Only the Lipan (li-PAHN) Apache stayed to fight, but the Comanche pushed them west off the plains. The Lipan worked with the Spanish, Mexicans, and Americans to fight the Comanche.

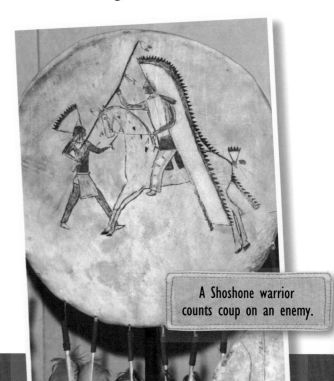

A Shoshone warrior counts coup on an enemy.

Lipan Apache warrior

Kiowa camp

In the early 1800s, the United States moved American Indian tribes to Indian Territory in Oklahoma. The Comanche attacked everyone who was on their land. But in 1835, the United States forced them to sign a **treaty**, promising to leave eastern American Indian groups alone.

Not all tribes saw the Comanche as enemies. The Kiowa (KAHY-uh-wuh) and Comanche once fought over land. But in 1805, a Kiowa warrior spent a summer with the Comanche. Over time, the two tribes made peace with each other.

Driven Off Their Land
The Caddo Leave Their Homeland

The French and Spanish had promised not to settle on Caddo land. After the Louisiana Purchase, the Caddo asked Americans to make the same promise. At first, Americans agreed to stay out of Caddo territory because they needed Caddo help in their boundary fights with Spain.

The Caddo also helped Americans fight against the British in the War of 1812. But after the United States won the war, they no longer needed Caddo help. Soon, settlers poured onto Caddo land.

Battle of New Orleans in the War of 1812

American Indian boys in boarding school

Boarding Schools

The United States forced American Indian children to attend boarding schools. The goal was to turn American Indian children into American citizens. Students could not speak their native language in school and had to wear American clothing. Many forgot their tribal customs.

Jose Maria

Jose Maria was the main Caddo chief from 1842 to 1862. He signed peace treaties with Texas and the United States. But he could not stop attacks from Comanche raiders and Texans. He finally agreed to move his people onto a reservation.

In 1845, Texas became part of the United States. Soon, the Caddo and other tribes moved to the Brazos Reservation. But Comanche raiders stole their horses. Texas settlers blamed the Caddo for the Comanche raids. In 1859, angry Texans tried to kill the Brazos Reservation Caddo. Finally, the Caddo moved to a reservation in Oklahoma.

Chief Jose Maria

Henry Dawes was the author of the Dawes General **Allotment** Act, or Dawes Act. He wanted to help American Indians. He thought the U. S. government should help to "civilize" them. Like most white Americans, Dawes thought that people needed to own property to be civilized. The Dawes Act was designed to civilize American Indians by dividing their land among themselves.

The act split up many reservation lands and divided them among adult males. Any remaining land could be sold to white settlers. But American Indians were used to sharing their land with one another. They had a hard time adjusting to the new lifestyle. By 1932, white settlers owned two-thirds of the original land in the Dawes Act.

The Comanche Give Up the Plains

The Comanche's rule over the plains ended with disease and war. Reservations and land laws took away their homes. Smallpox **epidemics** (ep-i-DEM-iks) in 1780 and 1816 wiped out entire Comanche bands. During the 1840s, California gold rushers came through the Comanchería, bringing another deadly wave of smallpox and **cholera** (KOL-er-uh) with them.

Many Comanche also died fighting Texas Rangers. Rangers were state lawmen. They protected settlers from American Indian raiders. But they did not keep people off Comanche land. The Rangers also took revenge when the Comanche attacked settlers on the Comanchería.

In 1867, most Comanche groups signed the Medicine Lodge Treaty. They gave up their land for a reservation in Oklahoma. The Kwahadi stayed on the plains. But they soon learned of a new enemy. American bison hunters killed millions of plains bison. The Kwahadi lost a fight against the hunters and the U. S. army. In 1875, the Kwahadi moved to a reservation.

The 1887 Dawes Act divided reservation lands. The goal of the act was to help American Indians to own their own land. But, in the end, it allowed white settlers to buy much of the land.

Dawes Act

the 1867 peace council at Medicine Lodge Creek

Keeping Their Cultures Alive
The Caddo Today

In 1928, a report linked American Indian poverty to land plots that could not be farmed. In 1934, Congress passed the Indian Reorganization Act. It stopped land allotments. It also returned reservation lands to American Indians. Many American Indian tribes became federally recognized tribes by the American government. This means they became free nations with their own laws. These tribes also receive special funding and land rights.

Caddo dancers

The Kadohadacho, Hasinai, and Natchitoches became federally recognized as the Caddo Indian Tribe of Oklahoma in 1938. The Caddo started their own tribal government. In 2002, they changed their name to The Caddo Nation of Oklahoma.

Today, many of the Caddo live in western Oklahoma. They gather to celebrate special events. They wear ancient Caddo clothes to festivals. They serve fried bread and other Caddo foods. The Caddo also sing and dance to their ancestors' songs. They work hard to keep the Caddo culture alive.

Chief White Bread

White Bread

White Bread was a respected Caddo leader from 1902 to 1913. He led Ghost Dance ceremonies. In these ceremonies, there was a Ghost Dance pole painted black for death and green for renewal. As a chief, White Bread often went to Washington, DC, to fight for Caddo rights.

Caddo Dances

The Turkey Dance is a women's dance that starts off every Caddo festival. Songs about Caddo history are sung during the Turkey Dance. Men and boys perform the Drum Dance in the evening. They carry a drum in a circle. They also sing songs about the beginning of Caddo people on Earth.

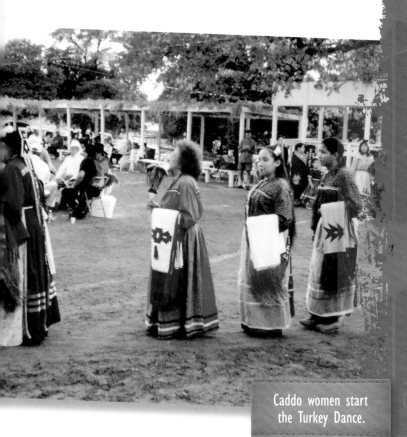

Caddo women start the Turkey Dance.

Keeping the Language Alive

In 1993, the Comanche Nation started the Comanche Language and Cultural Preservation Committee (CLCPC). Its mission is to keep the Comanche language alive. The CLCPC teaches Comanche people how to speak and write their language. It created an official Comanche alphabet in 1994.

Code Talkers

During the world wars, the United States trained American Indians as code talkers. Code talkers were soldiers who sent secret messages using codes based on American Indian languages. Fourteen Comanche soldiers served as code talkers. They used a code based on the Comanche language. The Comanche word for *turtle* meant "tank." *Pregnant airplane* meant "bomber."

The Comanche Today

In 1967, the Comanche were federally recognized as the Comanche Nation of Oklahoma. They wrote their own **constitution**, or set of laws. Today, there are around 20,000 Comanche in the United States. Half of them live on reservation lands in Southwest Oklahoma.

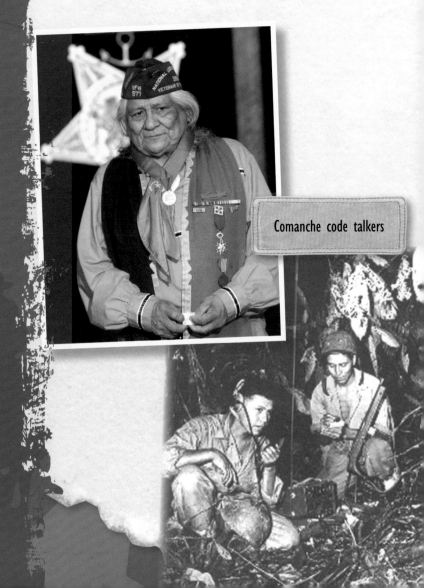

Comanche code talkers

The Comanche teach their children about their ancestors' way of life. The Comanche hold annual fairs. They enjoy traditional food, games, and music. The Comanche work hard to preserve their arts and language. They also protect their history and **landmarks**.

The Caddo and Comanche are Americans. They lead similar lives to other modern Americans. But they are also part of American Indian nations. They are direct **descendants** (dih-SEN-duhnts) of the first Americans. Their people survived war, disease, and the loss of their land. But the Caddo and Comanche still honor the earth and spirits. They are proud of their cultures and history and continue to pass them on to future generations.

Comanche boy

Glossary

alliances—associations of groups who agree to cooperate for common goals

allotment—a small section of land

archaeologists—scientists who study ancient people and cultures

breechcloths—cloths worn around the hips

cholera—an infection that causes severe stomach illness and sometimes death

colony—a country or area under the control of another country; a group of people living there

confederacies—united groups of American Indian tribes or bands

constitution—a written statement outlining the basic laws for a state or country

descendants—people who can trace their ancestors or lineage to a particular group

epidemics—widespread outbreaks of disease

fortified—protected or strengthened against attack

landmarks—important buildings or statues

matrilineal—passed down or inherited through the mother's family

moccasins—soft leather shoes without heels

mohawk—long strip of hair down the center of the head

nomadic—having no fixed home; moving with the seasons in search of food

reservations—areas of land set aside by the federal government for American Indians

scalps—skins covering the tops of heads that usually are covered with hair

smallpox—a disease caused by a virus; characterized by a fever and skin rash

tepees—cone-shaped tents used as shelter

tinkling—to make a series of ringing or clinking sounds

travois—a sled made of a frame and two poles that are attached to a horse

treaty—a legal agreement between two governments

turquoise—greenish blue semiprecious stone used in jewelry

worshipped—honored or adored something or someone, usually a god

Index

Your Turn!

American Indians were the first people to live in Texas. Two of
the main tribes in the region were the Caddo and Comanche.
The Caddo lived in East Texas in the Red River Valley. They
became expert farmers and traders. The Comanche were nomadic
hunters. They followed buffalo herds across the Texas plains.
They were expert horse trainers. They were also known for
raiding other tribes and white settlements.

Which One Would You Choose?

The Caddo and Comanche tribes were the first residents of Texas.
But their ways of life were very different. Which way of life would
you have liked better? Write a paragraph that explains the reasons
for your choice.